Louis Armstrong
American Musician

Kat Mellark

New York

Published in 2014 by The Rosen Publishing Group, Inc.
29 East 21st Street, New York, NY 10010

Book Design: Katelyn Londino

Photo Credits: Cover Eliot Elisofun/Time & Life Pictures/Getty Images; p. 5 WALTER SANDERS/Time & Life Pictures/Getty Images; p. 7 (cornet) en.wikipedia.org/wiki/File:Cornet-Bb-large.jpg/Wikipedia.org; p. 7 (Louis Armstrong) Frank Driggs/Michael Ochs Archives/Getty Images; pp. 9, 13 Frank Driggs Collection/Archive Photos/Getty Images; p. 11 Hulton Archive/Getty Images; p. 15 Michael Ochs Archives/Getty Images; p. 17 Ernst Haas/Getty Images; p. 19 Terrence Spencer/Time & Life Pictures/Getty Images; p. 22 Evening Standard/Hulton Archive/Getty Images.

ISBN: 978-1-4777-2428-6
6-pack ISBN: 978-1-4777-2429-3

Manufactured in the United States of America

CPSIA Compliance Information: Batch #CS13RC: For further information contact Rosen Publishing, New York, New York at 1-800-237-9932.

Contents

Growing Up

Louis Armstrong was born in New Orleans, Louisiana, in 1901. There were a lot of gangs in his neighborhood. His family was very poor, so Louis had to find ways to make money. Sometimes Louis, who liked to be called Louie, sang with his friends on street corners. New Orleans was a musical city. Louis learned a lot about music there.

New Orleans was the musical city Louis Armstrong was born in.

5

Louis stopped going to school after third grade. A few years later, he was sent to live at a home for troubled boys because he broke the law. While he was there, he was given his first music **lessons**. He played an **instrument** called the cornet. That's a small brass instrument with three keys.

Louis's first music lessons were given to him when he was at a home for troubled boys.

cornet

After a few years, Louis came back to live with his family. He'd been the leader of the band at the home for troubled boys. Now, he started to play with bands around New Orleans. Joe Oliver, a famous trumpet player, heard Louis play. He offered to give Louis music lessons.

The great trumpet player who offered to give Louis music lessons was named Joe Oliver.

Joe Oliver

On the River

In the early 1900s, **steamboats** were used to carry people up and down the Mississippi River. Sometimes people played music on these boats for money. Louis got his first real job on a steamboat. As he traveled on the steamboat, he learned more about music. He played different kinds of music and learned how to read it.

Many people traveled up and down the Mississippi River on big steamboats in the early 1900s.

11

The Hot Five

Joe Oliver didn't forget about Louis. He invited Louis to Chicago, Illinois, to play in his band. In Chicago, Louis played music with Joe, whom people called "King." After that, Louis made his own band, which he called the Hot Five. They recorded songs together. Louis was becoming famous!

The Hot Five was a famous jazz band that Louis Armstrong made on his own.

New York City

New York City was the home of some of the greatest jazz music. Great jazz **musicians** like Duke Ellington and Ella Fitzgerald made music there. By this time, Louis was famous for his music. He played his trumpet with many bands in New York City. He also recorded songs with other great jazz musicians.

Ella Fitzgerald was a great jazz musician. She made music with Louis Armstrong in New York City.

Ella Fitzgerald

15

Louis Armstrong made scat singing **popular** in jazz. Scat singing is when someone sings without using full words. It's like using the mouth as an instrument. Louis sang songs with words, too. People loved his deep voice. His voice was unlike any other singer's voice.

Scat singing became popular in jazz because of Louis Armstrong's way of singing without words.

Traveling

Louis brought his music with him wherever he went. He traveled all over the United States, especially in the South. Then, he traveled all over Europe to countries like Italy, France, and Germany. He even traveled to Africa! He helped spread jazz, a kind of music born in America, to the rest of the world.

Many people around the world knew about jazz because of Louis Armstrong's travels.

Louis is known by most people for his music. However, he was also an actor in over 20 movies! He acted in two very famous movies called *Hello, Dolly!* and *Pennies from Heaven*. Most of the characters he played in movies were also musicians. He helped bring jazz music to the movies.

The next page shows when many important events happened in Louis's life!

Life of a Jazz Star

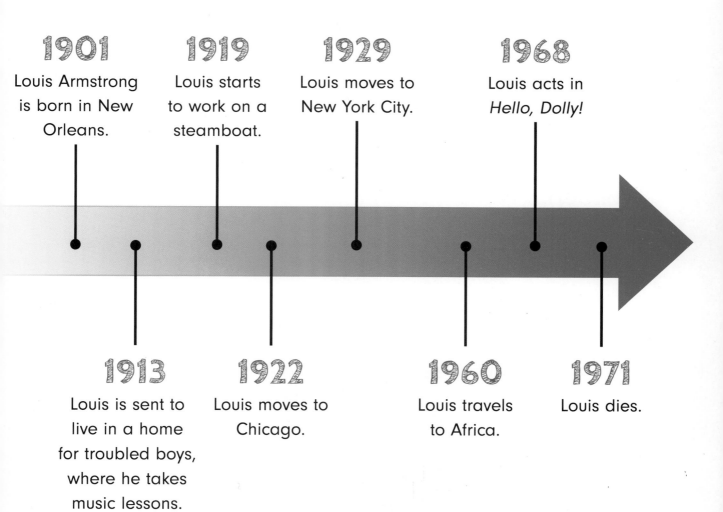

1901
Louis Armstrong is born in New Orleans.

1919
Louis starts to work on a steamboat.

1929
Louis moves to New York City.

1968
Louis acts in *Hello, Dolly!*

1913
Louis is sent to live in a home for troubled boys, where he takes music lessons.

1922
Louis moves to Chicago.

1960
Louis travels to Africa.

1971
Louis dies.

21

A Legacy

Louis Armstrong left behind a **legacy** of great music. He changed jazz music in America and showed it to the rest of the world. Today, many people know him for his deep voice and his songs, such as "What a Wonderful World." He will always be known as the father of jazz.

Glossary

instrument (IHN-struh-muhnt) Something used to make music.

legacy (LEH-guh-see) Something that is passed down after someone dies.

lesson (LEH-suhn) A meeting during which you learn something.

musician (myoo-ZIH-shuhn) A person who plays, sings, or writes music.

popular (PAH-pyuh-luhr) Liked by many people.

steamboat (STEEM-boht) A boat that runs on steam power.

Index